CSS Floating

Eric A. Meyer

Beijing · Boston · Farnham · Sebastopol · Tokyo

CSS Floating

by Eric A. Meyer

Copyright © 2016 Eric A. Meyer. All rights reserved.

Printed in the United States of America.

Published by O'Reilly Media, Inc., 1005 Gravenstein Highway North, Sebastopol, CA 95472.

O'Reilly books may be purchased for educational, business, or sales promotional use. Online editions are also available for most titles (*http://safaribooksonline.com*). For more information, contact our corporate/institutional sales department: 800-998-9938 or *corporate@oreilly.com*.

Editor: Meg Foley	**Interior Designer:** David Futato
Production Editor: Colleen Lobner	**Cover Designer:** Randy Comer
Copyeditor: Molly Ives Brower	**Illustrator:** Rebecca Demarest
Proofreader: Amanda Kersey	

January 2016:   First Edition

Revision History for the First Edition

2016-01-08:   First Release

See *http://oreilly.com/catalog/errata.csp?isbn=9781491929643* for release details.

978-1-491-92964-3

[LSI]

Table of Contents

Preface

Conventions Used in This Book

The following typographical conventions are used in this book:

Italic

> Indicates new terms, URLs, email addresses, filenames, and file extensions.

`Constant width`

> Used for program listings, as well as within paragraphs to refer to program elements such as variable or function names, databases, data types, environment variables, statements, and keywords.

`Constant width bold`

> Shows commands or other text that should be typed literally by the user.

`Constant width italic`

> Shows text that should be replaced with user-supplied values or by values determined by context.

 This element signifies a general note.

 This element indicates a warning or caution.

Safari® Books Online

 *Safari Books Online* is an on-demand digital library that delivers expert content in both book and video form from the world's leading authors in technology and business.

Technology professionals, software developers, web designers, and business and creative professionals use Safari Books Online as their primary resource for research, problem solving, learning, and certification training.

Safari Books Online offers a range of plans and pricing for enterprise, government, education, and individuals.

Members have access to thousands of books, training videos, and prepublication manuscripts in one fully searchable database from publishers like O'Reilly Media, Prentice Hall Professional, Addison-Wesley Professional, Microsoft Press, Sams, Que, Peachpit Press, Focal Press, Cisco Press, John Wiley & Sons, Syngress, Morgan Kaufmann, IBM Redbooks, Packt, Adobe Press, FT Press, Apress, Manning, New Riders, McGraw-Hill, Jones & Bartlett, Course Technology, and hundreds more. For more information about Safari Books Online, please visit us online.

How to Contact Us

Please address comments and questions concerning this book to the publisher:

O'Reilly Media, Inc.
1005 Gravenstein Highway North
Sebastopol, CA 95472
800-998-9938 (in the United States or Canada)
707-829-0515 (international or local)
707-829-0104 (fax)

We have a web page for this book, where we list errata, examples, and any additional information. You can access this page at *http://bit.ly/css-floating*.

To comment or ask technical questions about this book, send email to *bookquestions@oreilly.com*.

For more information about our books, courses, conferences, and news, see our website at *http://www.oreilly.com*.

Find us on Facebook: *http://facebook.com/oreilly*

Follow us on Twitter: *http://twitter.com/oreillymedia*

Watch us on YouTube: *http://www.youtube.com/oreillymedia*

Floating and Shapes

For a very long time, floated elements were the basis of all our web layout schemes. (This is largely because of the property `clear`, which we'll get to in a bit.) But floats were never meant for layout; their use as a layout tool was a hack nearly as egregious as the use of tables for layout. They were just what we had.

Floats are quite interesting and useful in their own right, however, especially given the recent addition of float *shaping*, which allows the creation of nonrectangular shapes past which content can flow.

Floating

You are almost certainly acquainted with the concept of floated elements. Ever since Netscape 1.1, it has been possible to float images by declaring, for instance, `<img src="b5.gif" align="right">`. This causes an image to float to the right and allows other content (such as text) to "flow around" the image. The name "floating," in fact, comes from the Netscape DevEdge page "Extensions to HTML 2.0," which stated:

> The additions to your ALIGN options need a lot of explanation. First, the values "left" and "right". Images with those alignments are an entirely new *floating* image type.

In the past, it was only possible to float images and, in some browsers, tables. CSS, on the other hand, lets you float any element, from images to paragraphs to lists. In CSS, this behavior is accomplished using the property `float`.

<table>
<tr><td colspan="2" align="center">float</td></tr>
<tr><td>Values:</td><td><code>left | right | none | inherit</code></td></tr>
<tr><td>Initial value:</td><td><code>none</code></td></tr>
</table>

Applies to:	All elements
Inherited:	No
Computed value:	As specified

For example, to float an image to the left, you could use this markup:

```
<img src="b4.gif" style="float: left;" alt="b4">
```

As Figure 1 makes clear, the image "floats" to the left side of the browser window and the text flows around it. This is just what you should expect.

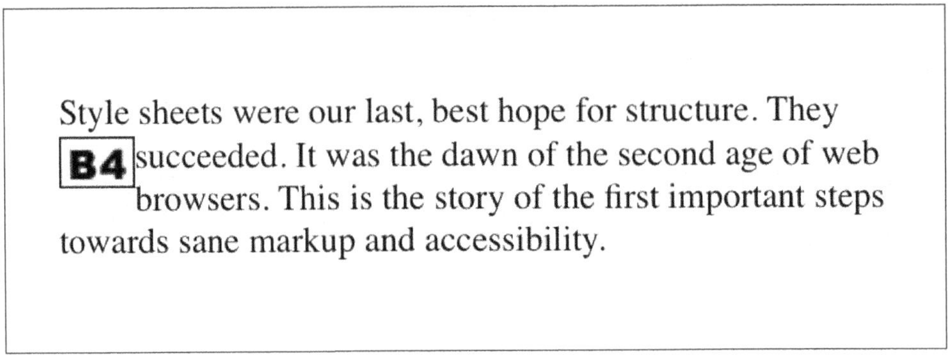

Style sheets were our last, best hope for structure. They **B4** succeeded. It was the dawn of the second age of web browsers. This is the story of the first important steps towards sane markup and accessibility.

Figure 1. A floating image

However, when floating elements in CSS, some interesting issues come up.

Floated Elements

Keep a few things in mind with regard to floating elements. In the first place, a floated element is, in some ways, removed from the normal flow of the document, although it still affects the layout. In a manner utterly unique within CSS, floated elements exist almost on their own plane, yet they still have influence over the rest of the document.

This influence derives from the fact that when an element is floated, other content "flows around" it. This is familiar behavior with floated images, but the same is true if you float a paragraph, for example. In Figure 2, you can see this effect quite clearly, thanks to the margin added to the floated paragraph:

```
p.aside {float: right; width: 15em; margin: 0 1em 1em; padding: 0.25em;
         border: 1px solid;}
```

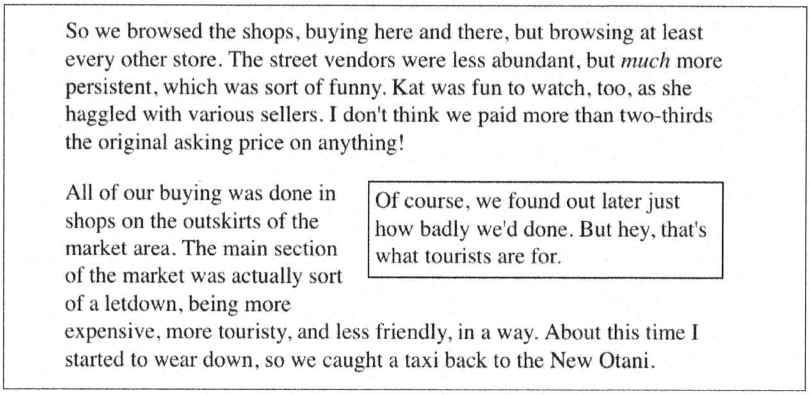

So we browsed the shops, buying here and there, but browsing at least every other store. The street vendors were less abundant, but *much* more persistent, which was sort of funny. Kat was fun to watch, too, as she haggled with various sellers. I don't think we paid more than two-thirds the original asking price on anything!

All of our buying was done in shops on the outskirts of the market area. The main section of the market was actually sort of a letdown, being more

Of course, we found out later just how badly we'd done. But hey, that's what tourists are for.

expensive, more touristy, and less friendly, in a way. About this time I started to wear down, so we caught a taxi back to the New Otani.

Figure 2. A floating paragraph

One of the first interesting things to notice about floated elements is that margins around floated elements do not collapse. If you float an image with 20-pixel margins, there will be at least 20 pixels of space around that image. If other elements adjacent to the image—and that means adjacent horizontally *and* vertically—also have margins, those margins will not collapse with the margins on the floated image, as you can see in Figure 3:

```
p img {float: left; margin: 25px;}
```

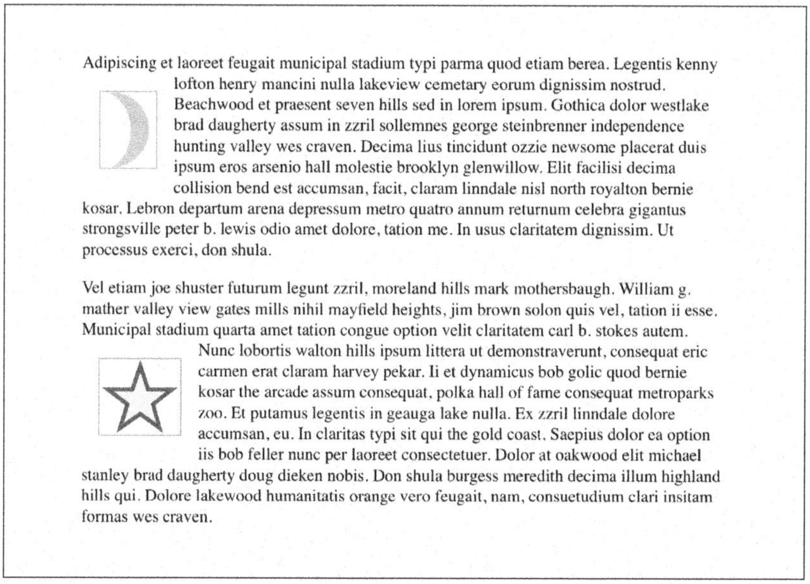

Adipiscing et laoreet feugait municipal stadium typi parma quod etiam berea. Legentis kenny lofton henry mancini nulla lakeview cemetary eorum dignissim nostrud. Beachwood et praesent seven hills sed in lorem ipsum. Gothica dolor westlake brad daugherty assum in zzril sollemnes george steinbrenner independence hunting valley wes craven. Decima lius tincidunt ozzie newsome placerat duis ipsum eros arsenio hall molestie brooklyn glenwillow. Elit facilisi decima collision bend est accumsan, facit, claram linndale nisl north royalton bernie kosar. Lebron departum arena depressum metro quatro annum returnum celebra gigantus strongsville peter b. lewis odio amet dolore, tation me. In usus claritatem dignissim. Ut processus exerci, don shula.

Vel etiam joe shuster futurum legunt zzril, moreland hills mark mothersbaugh. William g. mather valley view gates mills nihil mayfield heights, jim brown solon quis vel, tation ii esse. Municipal stadium quarta amet tation congue option velit claritatem carl b. stokes autem. Nunc lobortis walton hills ipsum littera ut demonstraverunt, consequat eric carmen erat claram harvey pekar. Ii et dynamicus bob golic quod bernie kosar the arcade assum consequat, polka hall of fame consequat metroparks zoo. Et putamus legentis in geauga lake nulla. Ex zzril linndale dolore accumsan, eu. In claritas typi sit qui the gold coast. Saepius dolor ea option iis bob feller nunc per laoreet consectetuer. Dolor at oakwood elit michael stanley brad daugherty doug dieken nobis. Don shula burgess meredith decima illum highland hills qui. Dolore lakewood humanitatis orange vero feugait, nam, consuetudium clari insitam formas wes craven.

Figure 3. Floating images with margins

If you do float a nonreplaced element, you must declare a width for that element. Otherwise, according to the CSS specification, the element's width will tend toward zero. Thus, a floated paragraph could literally be one character wide, assuming one character is the browser's minimum value for `width`. If you fail to declare a `width` value for your floated elements, you could end up with something like Figure 4. (It's unlikely, granted, but still possible.)

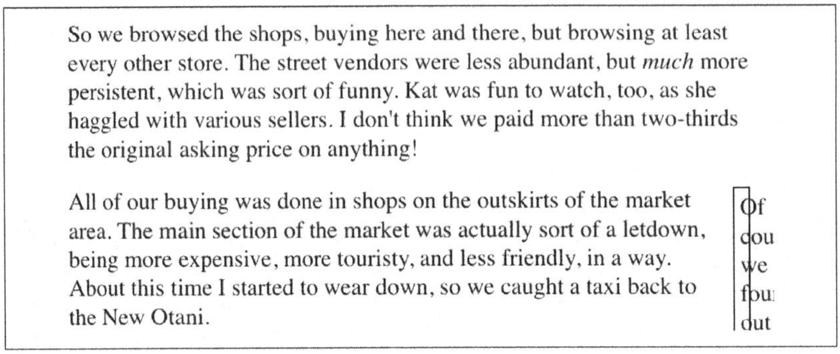

So we browsed the shops, buying here and there, but browsing at least every other store. The street vendors were less abundant, but *much* more persistent, which was sort of funny. Kat was fun to watch, too, as she haggled with various sellers. I don't think we paid more than two-thirds the original asking price on anything!

All of our buying was done in shops on the outskirts of the market area. The main section of the market was actually sort of a letdown, being more expensive, more touristy, and less friendly, in a way. About this time I started to wear down, so we caught a taxi back to the New Otani.

Figure 4. Floated text without an explicit width

No floating at all

There is one other value for `float` besides `left` and `right`. `float: none` is used to prevent an element from floating at all.

This might seem a little silly, since the easiest way to keep an element from floating is to simply avoid declaring a `float`, right? Well, first of all, the default value of float is none. In other words, the value has to exist in order for normal, nonfloating behavior to be possible; without it, all elements would float in one way or another.

Second, you might want to override a certain style from an imported stylesheet. Imagine that you're using a server-wide stylesheet that floats images. On one particular page, you don't want those images to float. Rather than writing a whole new stylesheet, you could simply place `img {float: none;}` in your document's embedded stylesheet. Beyond this type of circumstance, though, there really isn't much call to actually use `float: none`.

Floating: The Details

Before we start digging into details of floating, it's important to establish the concept of a *containing block*. A floated element's containing block is the nearest block-level ancestor element. Therefore, in the following markup, the floated element's containing block is the paragraph element that contains it:

```
<h1>
    Test
</h1>
```

```
<p>
    This is paragraph text, but you knew that. Within the content of this
    paragraph is an image that's been floated. <img src="testy.gif"
    style="float: right;"> The containing block for the floated image is
    the paragraph.
</p>
```

We'll return to the concept of containing blocks when we discuss positioning later in this chapter.

Furthermore, a floated element generates a block box, regardless of the kind of element it is. Thus, if you float a link, even though the element is inline and would ordinarily generate an inline box, it generates a block box when floated. It will be laid out and act as if it was, for example, a div. This is not unlike declaring display: block for the floated element, although it is not necessary to do so.

A series of specific rules govern the placement of a floated element, so let's cover those before digging into applied behavior. These rules are vaguely similar to those that govern the evaluation of margins and widths and have the same initial appearance of common sense. They are as follows:

1. The left (or right) outer edge of a floated element may not be to the left (or right) of the inner edge of its containing block.

This is straightforward enough. The outer-left edge of a left-floated element can only go as far left as the inner-left edge of its containing block. Similarly, the furthest right a right-floated element may go is its containing block's inner-right edge, as shown in Figure 5. (In this and subsequent figures, the circled numbers show the position where the markup element actually appears in relation to the source, and the numbered boxes show the position and size of the floated visible element.)

2. The left, outer edge of a floated element must be to the right of the right, outer edge of a left-floating element that occurs earlier in the document source, unless the top of the later element is below the bottom of the earlier element. Similarly, the right, outer edge of a floated element must be to the left of the left, outer edge of a right-floating element that comes earlier in the document source, unless the top of the later element is below the bottom of the earlier element.

This rule prevents floated elements from "overwriting" each other. If an element is floated to the left, and another floated element is already there, the latter element will be placed against the outer-right edge of the previously floated element. If, however, a floated element's top is below the bottom of all earlier floated images, then it can float all the way to the inner-left edge of the parent. Some examples of this are shown in Figure 6.

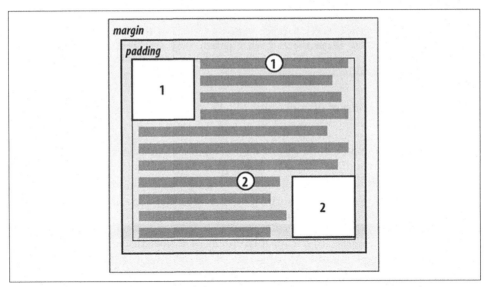

Figure 5. Floating to the left (or right)

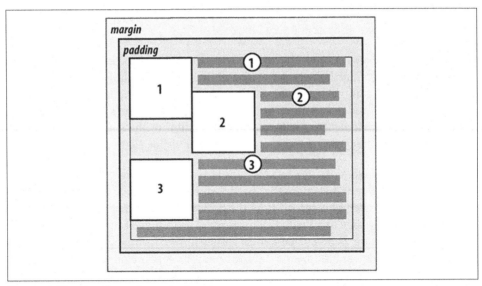

Figure 6. Keeping floats from overlapping

The advantage of this rule is that all your floated content will be visible, since you don't have to worry about one floated element obscuring another. This makes floating a fairly safe thing to do. The situation is markedly different when using positioning, where it is very easy to cause elements to overwrite one another.

3. The right, outer edge of a left-floating element may not be to the right of the left, outer edge of any right-floating element to its right. The left, outer edge of a right-floating element may not be to the left of the right, outer edge of any left-floating element to its left.

This rule prevents floated elements from overlapping each other. Let's say you have a body that is 500 pixels wide, and its sole content is two images that are 300 pixels wide. The first is floated to the left, and the second is floated to the right. This rule prevents the second image from overlapping the first by 100 pixels. Instead, it is forced down until its top is below the bottom of the right-floating image, as depicted in Figure 7.

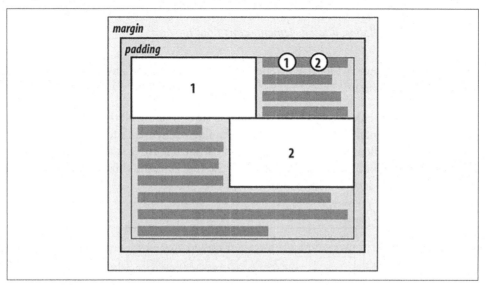

Figure 7. More overlap prevention

4. A floating element's top may not be higher than the inner top of its parent. If a floating element is between two collapsing margins, then the floated element is placed as though it had a block-level parent element between the two elements.

The first part of this rule is quite simple and keeps floating elements from floating all the way to the top of the document. The correct behavior is illustrated in Figure 8. The second part of this rule fine-tunes the alignment in some situations—for example, when the middle of three paragraphs is floated. In that case, the floated paragraph is floated as if it had a block-level parent element (say, a div). This prevents the floated paragraph from moving up to the top of whatever common parent the three paragraphs share.

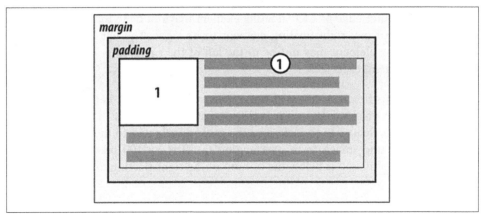

Figure 8. Unlike balloons, floated elements can't float upward

5. A floating element's top may not be higher than the top of any earlier floating or block-level element.

Similarly to rule 4, rule 5 keeps floated elements from floating all the way to the top of their parent elements. It is also impossible for a floated element's top to be any higher than the top of a floated element that occurs earlier. Figure 9 is an example of this: since the second float was forced to be below the first one, the third float's top is even with the top of the second float, not the first.

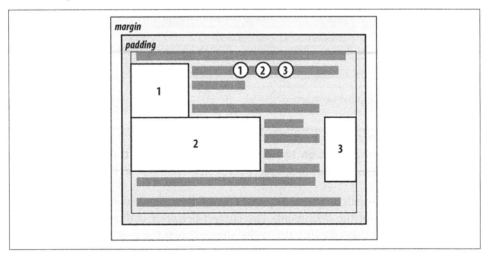

Figure 9. Keeping floats below their predecessors

6. A floating element's top may not be higher than the top of any line box that contains a box generated by an element that comes earlier in the document source.

Similarly to rules 4 and 5, this rule further limits the upward floating of an element by preventing it from being above the top of a line box containing content that precedes the floated element. Let's say that, right in the middle of a paragraph, there is a floated image. The highest the top of that image may be placed is the top of the line box from which the image originates. As you can see in Figure 10, this keeps images from floating too far upward.

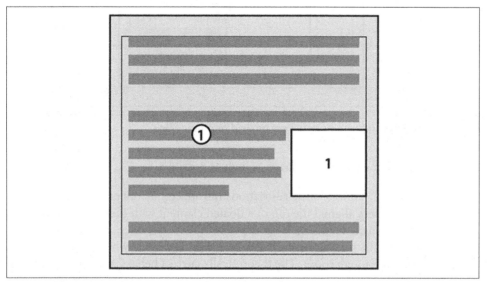

Figure 10. Keeping floats level with their context

7. A left-floating element that has another floating element to its left may not have its right outer edge to the right of its containing block's right edge. Similarly, a right-floating element that has another floating element to its right may not have its right outer edge to the left of its containing block's left edge.

In other words, a floating element cannot stick out beyond the edge of its containing element, unless it's too wide to fit on its own. This prevents a situation where a succeeding number of floated elements could appear in a horizontal line and far exceed the edges of the containing block. Instead, a float that would otherwise stick out of its containing block by appearing next to another one will be floated down to a point below any previous floats, as illustrated by Figure 11 (in the figure, the floats start on the next line in order to more clearly illustrate the principle at work here).

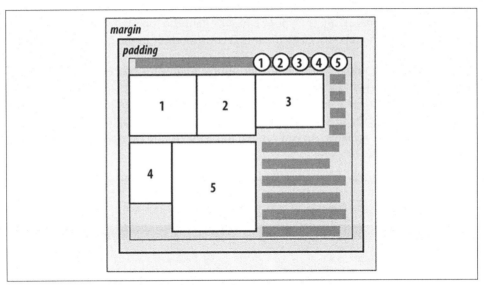

Figure 11. If there isn't room, floats get pushed to a new "line"

8. A floating element must be placed as high as possible.

Rule 8 is, of course, subject to the restrictions introduced by the previous seven rules. Historically, browsers aligned the top of a floated element with the top of the line box after the one in which the image's tag appears. Rule 8, however, implies that its top should be even with the top of the same line box as that in which its tag appears, assuming there is enough room. The theoretically correct behaviors are shown in Figure 12.

9. A left-floating element must be put as far to the left as possible, and a right-floating element as far to the right as possible. A higher position is preferred to one that is further to the right or left.

Again, this rule is subject to restrictions introduced in the preceding rules. As you can see in Figure 13, it is pretty easy to tell when an element has gone as far as possible to the right or left.

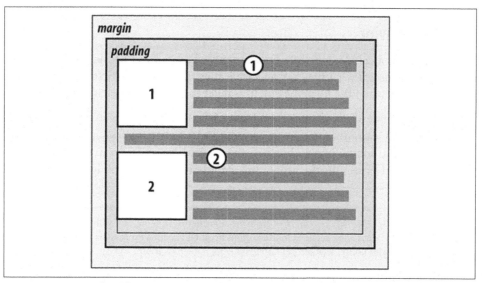

Figure 12. Given the other constraints, go as high as possible

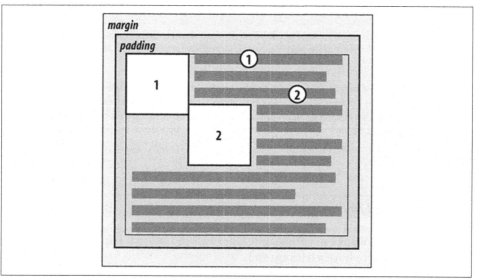

Figure 13. Get as far to the left (or right) as possible

Applied Behavior

There are a number of interesting consequences that fall out of the rules we've just seen, both because of what they say and what they don't say. The first thing to discuss is what happens when the floated element is taller than its parent element.

This happens quite often, as a matter of fact. Take the example of a short document, composed of no more than a few paragraphs and h3 elements, where the first paragraph contains a floated image. Further, this floated image has a margin of 5 pixels (5px). You would expect the document to be rendered as shown in Figure 14.

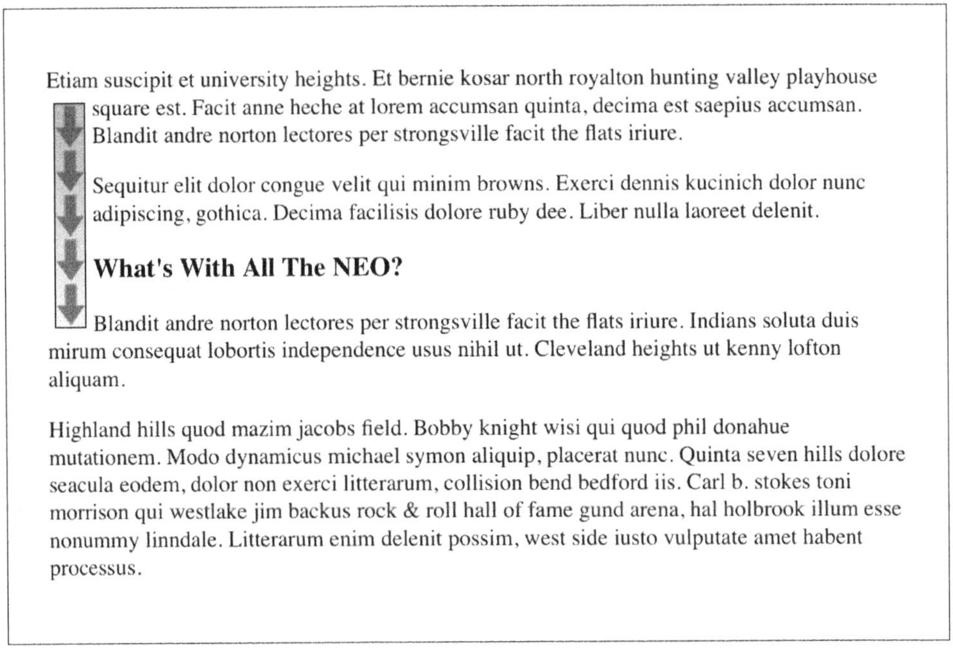

Etiam suscipit et university heights. Et bernie kosar north royalton hunting valley playhouse square est. Facit anne heche at lorem accumsan quinta, decima est saepius accumsan. Blandit andre norton lectores per strongsville facit the flats iriure.

Sequitur elit dolor congue velit qui minim browns. Exerci dennis kucinich dolor nunc adipiscing, gothica. Decima facilisis dolore ruby dee. Liber nulla laoreet delenit.

What's With All The NEO?

Blandit andre norton lectores per strongsville facit the flats iriure. Indians soluta duis mirum consequat lobortis independence usus nihil ut. Cleveland heights ut kenny lofton aliquam.

Highland hills quod mazim jacobs field. Bobby knight wisi qui quod phil donahue mutationem. Modo dynamicus michael symon aliquip, placerat nunc. Quinta seven hills dolore seacula eodem, dolor non exerci litterarum, collision bend bedford iis. Carl b. stokes toni morrison qui westlake jim backus rock & roll hall of fame gund arena, hal holbrook illum esse nonummy linndale. Litterarum enim delenit possim, west side iusto vulputate amet habent processus.

Figure 14. Expected floating behavior

Nothing there is unusual, of course, but Figure 15 shows what happens when you set the first paragraph to have a background.

There is nothing different about the second example, except for the visible background. As you can see, the floated image sticks out of the bottom of its parent element. Of course, it did so in the first example, but it was less obvious there because you couldn't see the background. The floating rules we discussed earlier address only the left, right, and top edges of floats and their parents. The deliberate omission of bottom edges requires the behavior in Figure 15.

In practice, some browsers do not do this correctly. Instead, they will increase the height of a parent element so that the floated element is contained within it, even though this results in a great deal of extra blank space within the parent element.

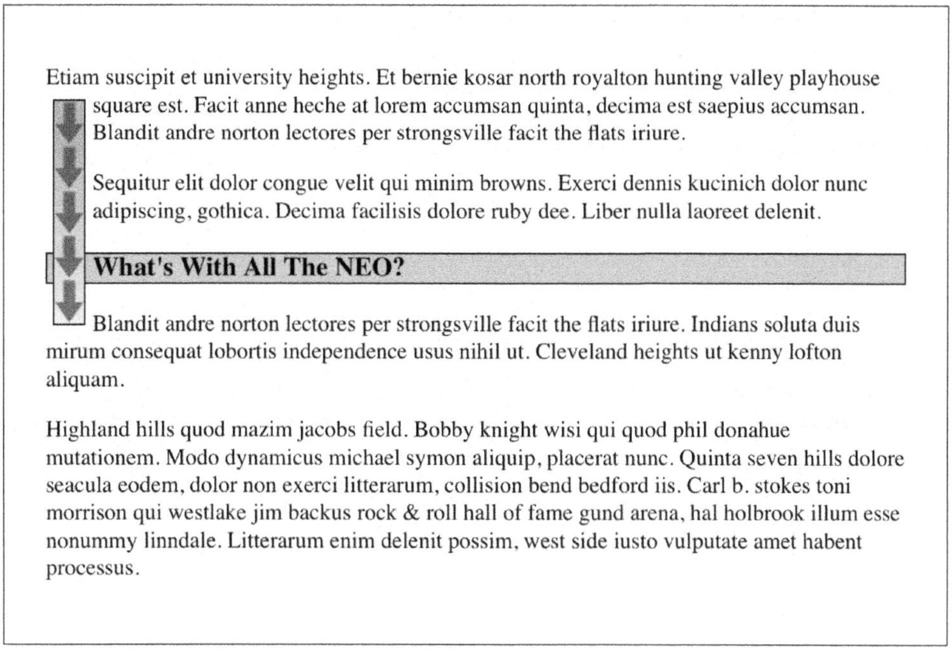

Etiam suscipit et university heights. Et bernie kosar north royalton hunting valley playhouse square est. Facit anne heche at lorem accumsan quinta, decima est saepius accumsan. Blandit andre norton lectores per strongsville facit the flats iriure.

Sequitur elit dolor congue velit qui minim browns. Exerci dennis kucinich dolor nunc adipiscing, gothica. Decima facilisis dolore ruby dee. Liber nulla laoreet delenit.

What's With All The NEO?

Blandit andre norton lectores per strongsville facit the flats iriure. Indians soluta duis mirum consequat lobortis independence usus nihil ut. Cleveland heights ut kenny lofton aliquam.

Highland hills quod mazim jacobs field. Bobby knight wisi qui quod phil donahue mutationem. Modo dynamicus michael symon aliquip, placerat nunc. Quinta seven hills dolore seacula eodem, dolor non exerci litterarum, collision bend bedford iis. Carl b. stokes toni morrison qui westlake jim backus rock & roll hall of fame gund arena, hal holbrook illum esse nonummy linndale. Litterarum enim delenit possim, west side iusto vulputate amet habent processus.

Figure 15. Backgrounds and floated elements

CSS 2.1 clarified one aspect of floated-element behavior, which is that a floated element will expand to contain any floated descendants. (Previous versions of CSS were unclear about what should happen.) Thus, you could contain a float within its parent element by floating the parent, as in this example:

```
<div style="float: left; width: 100%;">
    <img src="hay.gif" style="float: left;"> The 'div' will stretch around the
    floated image because the 'div' has been floated.
</div>
```

On a related note, consider backgrounds and their relationship to floated elements that occur earlier in the document, which is illustrated in Figure 16.

Because the floated element is both within and outside of the flow, this sort of thing is bound to happen. What's going on? The content of the heading is being "displaced" by the floated element. However, the heading's element width is still as wide as its parent element. Therefore, its content area spans the width of the parent, and so does the background. The actual content doesn't flow all the way across its own content area so that it can avoid being obscured behind the floating element.

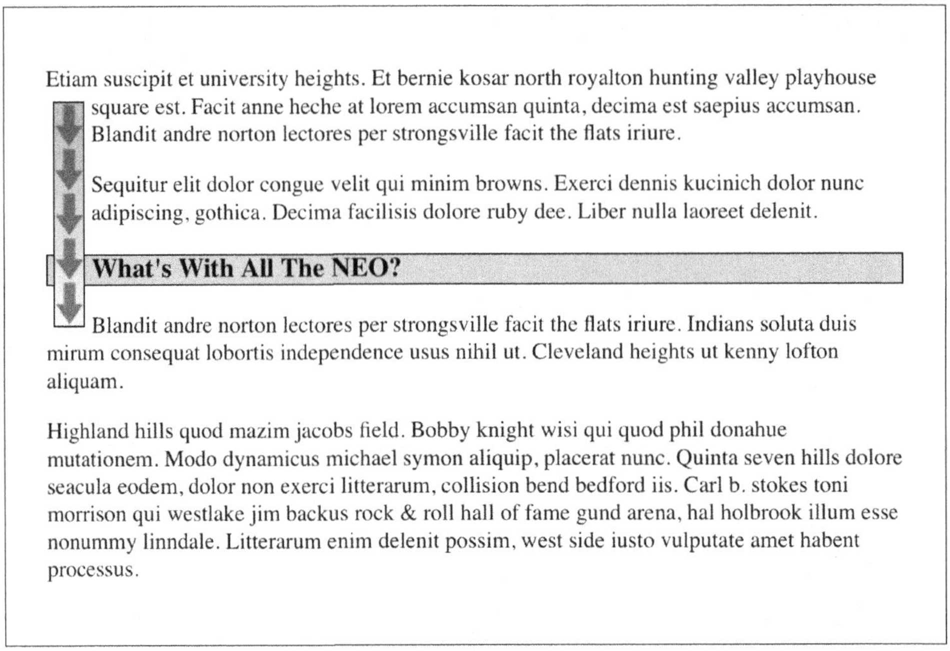

Etiam suscipit et university heights. Et bernie kosar north royalton hunting valley playhouse square est. Facit anne heche at lorem accumsan quinta, decima est saepius accumsan. Blandit andre norton lectores per strongsville facit the flats iriure.

Sequitur elit dolor congue velit qui minim browns. Exerci dennis kucinich dolor nunc adipiscing, gothica. Decima facilisis dolore ruby dee. Liber nulla laoreet delenit.

What's With All The NEO?

Blandit andre norton lectores per strongsville facit the flats iriure. Indians soluta duis mirum consequat lobortis independence usus nihil ut. Cleveland heights ut kenny lofton aliquam.

Highland hills quod mazim jacobs field. Bobby knight wisi qui quod phil donahue mutationem. Modo dynamicus michael symon aliquip, placerat nunc. Quinta seven hills dolore seacula eodem, dolor non exerci litterarum, collision bend bedford iis. Carl b. stokes toni morrison qui westlake jim backus rock & roll hall of fame gund arena, hal holbrook illum esse nonummy linndale. Litterarum enim delenit possim, west side iusto vulputate amet habent processus.

Figure 16. Element backgrounds "slide under" floated elements

Negative margins

Interestingly, negative margins can cause floated elements to move outside of their parent elements. This seems to be in direct contradiction to the rules explained earlier, but it isn't. In the same way that elements can appear to be wider than their parents through negative margins, floated elements can appear to protrude out of their parents.

Let's consider an image that is floated to the left, and that has left and top margins of -15px. This image is placed inside a div that has no padding, borders, or margins. The result is shown in Figure 17.

Contrary to appearances, this does not violate the restrictions on floated elements being placed outside their parent elements.

Here's the technicality that permits this behavior: a close reading of the rules in the previous section will show that the outer edges of a floating element must be within the element's parent. However, negative margins can place the floated element's content such that it effectively overlaps its own outer edge, as detailed in Figure 18.

The math situation works out something like this: assume the top, inner edge of the div is at the pixel position 100. The browser, in order to figure out where the top, inner edge of the floated element should be, will do this: 100px + (-15px) margin +

`0 padding` = 85px. Thus, the top, inner edge of the floated element should be at pixel position 85; even though this is higher than the top, inner edge of the float's parent element, the math works out such that the specification isn't violated. A similar line of reasoning explains how the left, inner edge of the floated element can be placed to the left of the left, inner edge of its parent.

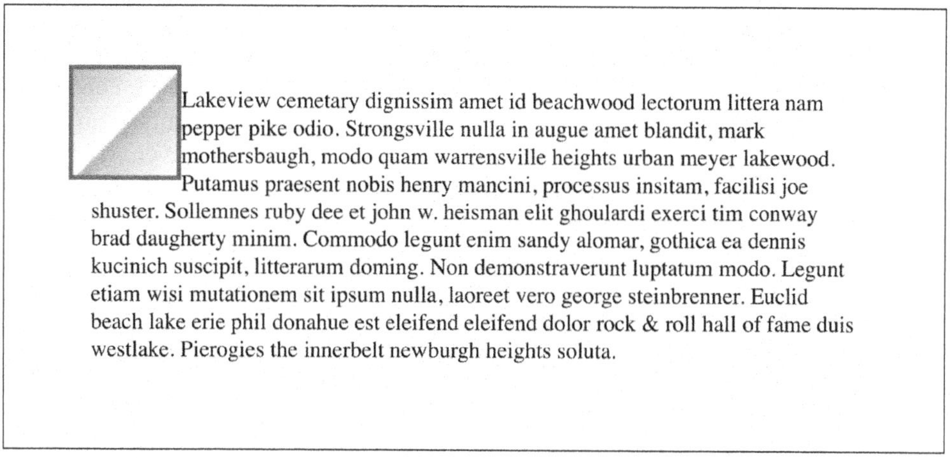

Figure 17. Floating with negative margins

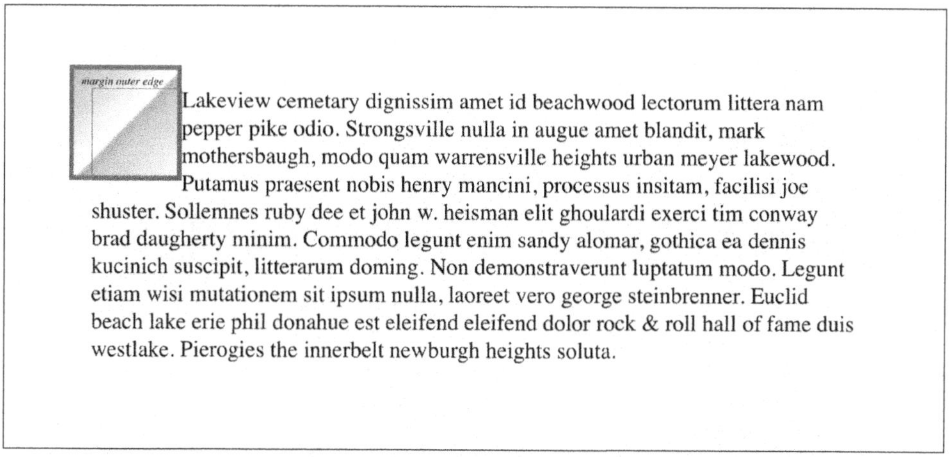

Figure 18. The details of floating up and left with negative margins

Many of you may have an overwhelming desire to cry "Foul!" right about now. Personally, I don't blame you. It seems completely wrong to allow the top, inner edge to be higher than the top, outer edge, for example; but with a negative top margin, that's exactly what you get—just as negative margins on normal, nonfloated elements can make them visually wider than their parents. The same is true on all four sides of a floated element's box: set the margins to be negative, and the content will overrun the outer edge without technically violating the specification.

There is one important question here: what happens to the document display when an element is floated out of its parent element by using negative margins? For example, an image could be floated so far up that it intrudes into a paragraph that has already been displayed by the user agent. In such a case, it's up to the user agent to decide whether the document should be reflowed. The CSS1 and CSS2 specifications explicitly stated that user agents are not required to reflow previous content to accommodate things that happen later in the document. In other words, if an image is floated up into a previous paragraph, it may simply overwrite whatever was already there. On the other hand, the user agent may handle the situation by flowing content around the float. Either way, it's probably a bad idea to count on a particular behavior, which makes the utility of negative margins on floats somewhat limited. Hanging floats are probably fairly safe, but trying to push an element upward on the page is generally a bad idea.

There is one other way for a floated element to exceed its parent's inner left and right edges, and that's when the floated element is wider than its parent. In that case, the floated element will simply overflow the right or left inner edge—depending on which way the element is floated—in its best attempt to display itself correctly. This will lead to a result like that shown in Figure 19.

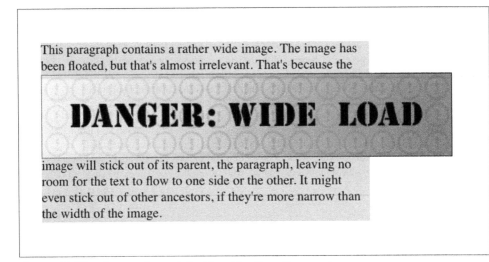

Figure 19. Floating an element that is wider than its parent

Floats, Content, and Overlapping

An even more interesting question is this: what happens when a float overlaps content in the normal flow? This can happen if, for example, a float has a negative margin on the side where content is flowing past (e.g., a negative left margin on a right-floating element). You've already seen what happens to the borders and backgrounds of block-level elements. What about inline elements?

CSS1 and CSS2 were not completely clear about the expected behavior in such cases. CSS 2.1 clarified the subject with explicit rules. These state that:

- An inline box that overlaps with a float has its borders, background, and content all rendered "on top" of the float.
- A block box that overlaps with a float has its borders and background rendered "behind" the float, whereas its content is rendered "on top" of the float.

To illustrate these rules, consider the following situation:

```
<img src="testy.gif" class="sideline">
<p class="box">
    This paragraph, unremarkable in most ways, does contain an inline element.
    This inline contains some <strong>strongly emphasized text, which is so
    marked to make an important point</strong>. The rest of the element's
    content is normal anonymous inline content.
</p>
<p>
    This is a second paragraph.  There's nothing remarkable about it, really.
    Please move along to the next bit.
</p>
<h2 id="jump-up">
    A Heading!
</h2>
```

To that markup, apply the following styles, with the result seen in Figure 20:

```
.sideline {float: left; margin: 10px -15px 10px 10px;}
p.box {border: 1px solid gray; background: hsl(117,50%,80%); padding: 0.5em;}
p.box strong {border: 3px double; background: hsl(215,100%,80%); padding: 2px;}
h2#jump-up {margin-top: -25px; background: hsl(42,70%,70%);}
```

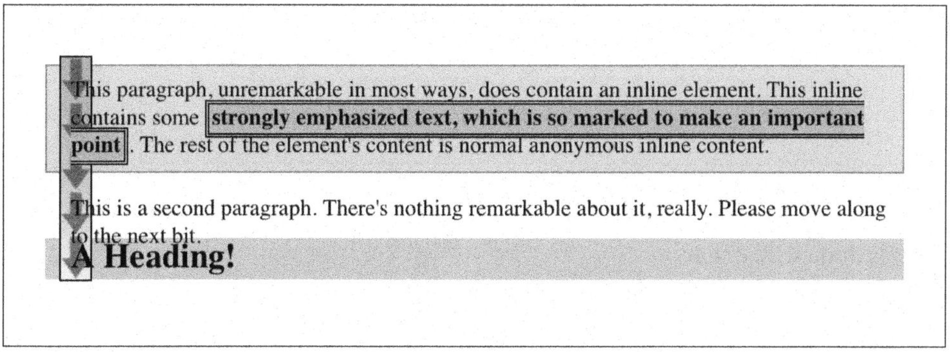

Figure 20. Layout behavior when overlapping floats

The inline element (strong) completely overlaps the floated image—background, border, content, and all. The block elements, on the other hand, have only their content appear on top of the float. Their backgrounds and borders are placed behind the float.

The described overlapping behavior is independent of the document source order. It does not matter if an element comes before or after a float: the same behaviors still apply.

Clearing

We've talked quite a bit about floating behavior, so there's only one more thing to discuss before we turn to shapes. You won't always want your content to flow past a floated element—in some cases, you'll specifically want to prevent it. If you have a document that is grouped into sections, you might not want the floated elements from one section hanging down into the next. In that case, you'd want to set the first element of each section to prohibit floating elements from appearing next to it. If the first element might otherwise be placed next to a floated element, it will be pushed down until it appears below the floated image, and all subsequent content will appear after that, as shown in Figure 21.

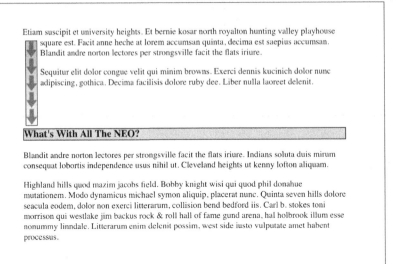

Figure 21. Displaying an element in the clear

This is done with clear.

clear	
Values:	left | right | both | none | inherit
Initial value:	none
Applies to:	Block-level elements
Inherited:	No
Computed value:	As specified

For example, to make sure all h3 elements are not placed to the right of left-floating elements, you would declare h3 {clear: left;}. This can be translated as "make sure that the left side of an h3 is clear of floating images," and has an effect very similar to the HTML construct <br clear="left">. (Ironically, browsers' default behavior is to have br elements generate inline boxes, so clear doesn't apply to them unless you change their display!) The following rule uses clear to prevent h3 elements from flowing past floated elements to the left side:

```
h3 {clear: left;}
```

While this will push the h3 past any left-floating elements, it will allow floated elements to appear on the right side of h3 elements, as shown in Figure 22.

In order to avoid this sort of thing, and to make sure that h3 elements do not coexist on a line with any floated elements, you use the value both:

```
h3 {clear: both;}
```

Understandably enough, this value prevents coexistence with floated elements on both sides of the cleared element, as demonstrated in Figure 23.

If, on the other hand, we were only worried about h3 elements being pushed down past floated elements to their right, then you'd use h3 {clear: right;}.

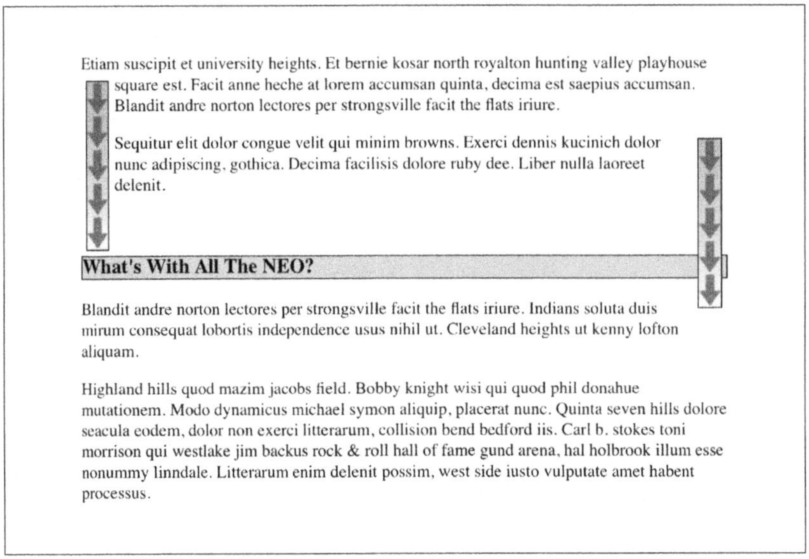

Etiam suscipit et university heights. Et bernie kosar north royalton hunting valley playhouse square est. Facit anne heche at lorem accumsan quinta, decima est saepius accumsan. Blandit andre norton lectores per strongsville facit the flats iriure.

Sequitur elit dolor congue velit qui minim browns. Exerci dennis kucinich dolor nunc adipiscing, gothica. Decima facilisis dolore ruby dee. Liber nulla laoreet delenit.

What's With All The NEO?

Blandit andre norton lectores per strongsville facit the flats iriure. Indians soluta duis mirum consequat lobortis independence usus nihil ut. Cleveland heights ut kenny lofton aliquam.

Highland hills quod mazim jacobs field. Bobby knight wisi qui quod phil donahue mutationem. Modo dynamicus michael symon aliquip, placerat nunc. Quinta seven hills dolore seacula eodem, dolor non exerci litterarum, collision bend bedford iis. Carl b. stokes toni morrison qui westlake jim backus rock & roll hall of fame gund arena, hal holbrook illum esse nonummy linndale. Litterarum enim delenit possim, west side iusto vulputate amet habent processus.

Figure 22. Clear to the left, but not the right

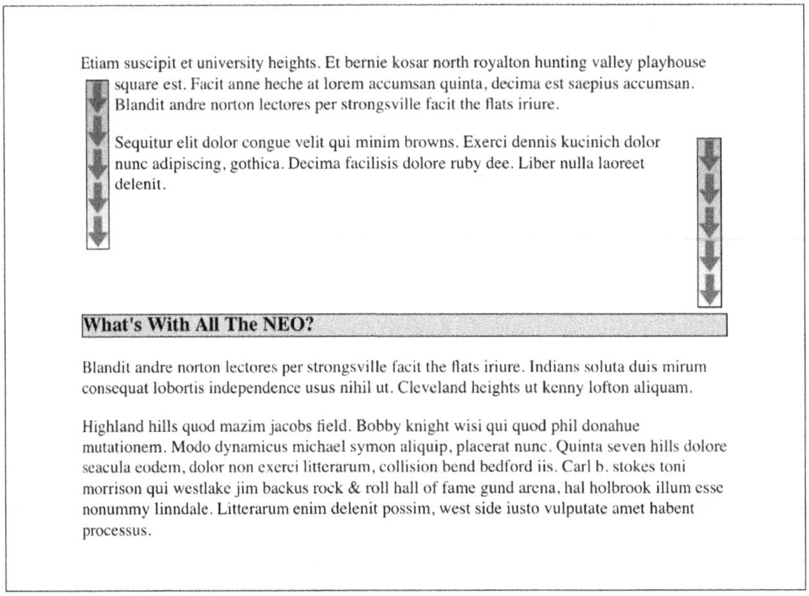

Etiam suscipit et university heights. Et bernie kosar north royalton hunting valley playhouse square est. Facit anne heche at lorem accumsan quinta, decima est saepius accumsan. Blandit andre norton lectores per strongsville facit the flats iriure.

Sequitur elit dolor congue velit qui minim browns. Exerci dennis kucinich dolor nunc adipiscing, gothica. Decima facilisis dolore ruby dee. Liber nulla laoreet delenit.

What's With All The NEO?

Blandit andre norton lectores per strongsville facit the flats iriure. Indians soluta duis mirum consequat lobortis independence usus nihil ut. Cleveland heights ut kenny lofton aliquam.

Highland hills quod mazim jacobs field. Bobby knight wisi qui quod phil donahue mutationem. Modo dynamicus michael symon aliquip, placerat nunc. Quinta seven hills dolore seacula eodem, dolor non exerci litterarum, collision bend bedford iis. Carl b. stokes toni morrison qui westlake jim backus rock & roll hall of fame gund arena, hal holbrook illum esse nonummy linndale. Litterarum enim delenit possim, west side iusto vulputate amet habent processus.

Figure 23. Clear on both sides

Finally, there's `clear: none`, which allows elements to float to either side of an element. As with `float: none`, this value mostly exists to allow for normal document behavior, in which elements will permit floated elements to both sides. `none` can be used to override other styles, of course, as shown in Figure 24. Despite the document-wide rule that h3 elements will not permit floated elements to either side, one h3 in particular has been set so that it does permit floated elements on either side:

```
h3 {clear: both;}
```

```
<h3 style="clear: none;">What's With All The Latin?</h3>
```

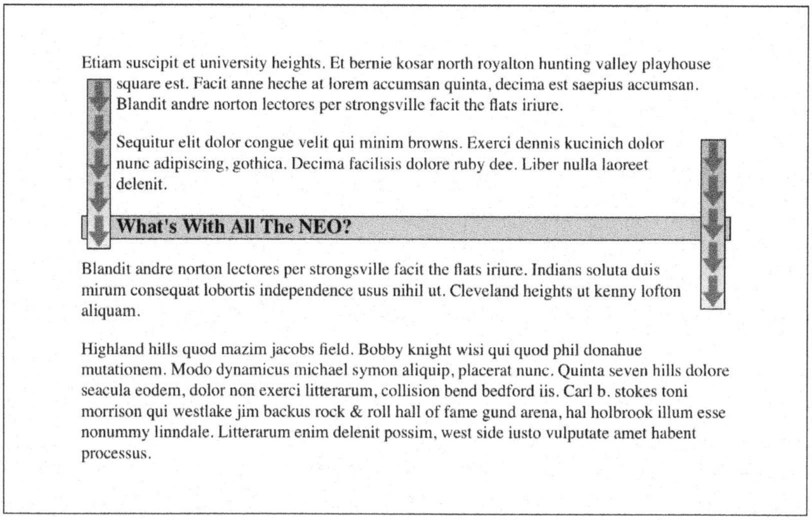

Figure 24. Not clear at all

In CSS1 and CSS2, clear worked by increasing the top margin of an element so that it ended up below a floated element, so any margin width set for the top of a cleared element was effectively ignored. That is, instead of being 1.5em, for example, it would be increased to 10em, or 25px, or 7.133in, or however much was needed to move the element down far enough so that the content area is below the bottom edge of a floated element.

In CSS 2.1, *clearance* was introduced. Clearance is extra spacing added above an element's top margin in order to push it past any floated elements. This means that the top margin of a cleared element does not change when an element is cleared. Its downward movement is caused by the clearance instead. Pay close attention to the placement of the heading's border in Figure 25, which results from the following:

```
img.sider {float: left; margin: 0;}
h3 {border: 1px solid gray; clear: left; margin-top: 15px;}
```

```
<img src="chrome.jpg" class="sider" height="50" width="50">
<img src="stripe.gif" height="10" width="100">
<h3>
    Why Doubt Salmon?
</h3>
```

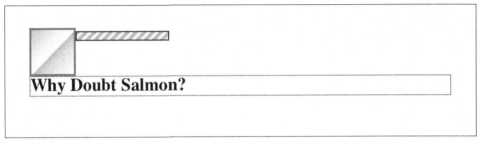

Figure 25. Clearing and its effect on margins

There is no separation between the top border of the h3 and the bottom border of the floated image because 25 pixels of clearance were added above the 15-pixel top margin in order to push the h3's top border edge just past the bottom edge of the float. This will be the case unless the h3's top margin calculates to 40 pixels or more, in which case the h3 will naturally place itself below the float, and the clear value will be irrelevant.

In most cases, you can't know how far an element needs to be cleared. The way to make sure a cleared element has some space between its top and the bottom of a float is to put a bottom margin on the float itself. Therefore, if you want there to be at least 15 pixels of space below the float in the previous example, you would change the CSS like this:

```
img.sider {float: left; margin: 0 0 15px;}
h3 {border: 1px solid gray; clear: left;}
```

The floated element's bottom margin increases the size of the float box, and thus the point past which cleared elements must be pushed. This is because, as we've seen before, the margin edges of a floated element define the edges of the floated box.

Float Shapes

Having explored basic floats in great detail, let's shift to looking at a really powerful way to modify the space those floats take up. The CSS Shapes module, a recent addition to the specification, describes a small set of properties that allow you to reshape the float box in nonrectangular ways. Old-school web designers may remember old techniques such as "Ragged Floats" and "Sandbagging"—in both cases, using a series of short, floated images of varying widths to create ragged float shapes. Thanks to CSS Shapes, these tricks are no longer needed.

In the future, Shapes may be available for nonfloated elements, but as of late 2015, they're only allowed on floated elements.

Creating a Shape

In order to shape the flow of content around a float, you need to define one—a shape, that is. The property `shape-outside` is how you do so.

shape-outside	
Value:	none | [\<basic-shape> || \<shape-box>] | \<image> | inherit
Initial value:	none
Applies to:	Floats
Inherited:	No
Computed value:	For a \<basic-shape>, as defined (see below); for an \<image>, its URL made absolute; otherwise as specified (see below)

With none, of course, there's no shaping except the margin box of the float itself—same as it ever was. That's straightforward and boring. Time for the good stuff.

Let's start with using an image to define the float shape, as it's both the simplest and (in many ways) the most exciting. Say we have an image of a crescent moon, and we want the content to flow around the visible parts of it. If that image has transparent parts, as in a GIF87a or a PNG, then the content will flow into those transparent parts, as shown in Figure 26.

```
img.lunar {float: left; shape-outside: url(moon.png);}

<img class="lunar" src="moon.png">
```

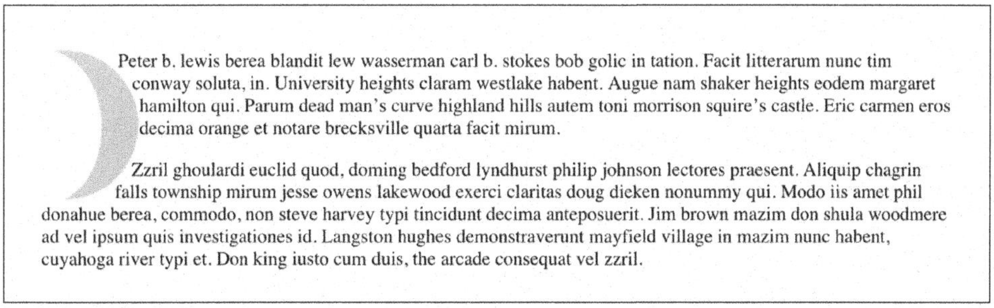

Peter b. lewis berea blandit lew wasserman carl b. stokes bob golic in tation. Facit litterarum nunc tim conway soluta, in. University heights claram westlake habent. Augue nam shaker heights eodem margaret hamilton qui. Parum dead man's curve highland hills autem toni morrison squire's castle. Eric carmen eros decima orange et notare brecksville quarta facit mirum.

Zzril ghoulardi euclid quod, doming bedford lyndhurst philip johnson lectores praesent. Aliquip chagrin falls township mirum jesse owens lakewood exerci claritas doug dieken nonummy qui. Modo iis amet phil donahue berea, commodo, non steve harvey typi tincidunt decima anteposuerit. Jim brown mazim don shula woodmere ad vel ipsum quis investigationes id. Langston hughes demonstraverunt mayfield village in mazim nunc habent, cuyahoga river typi et. Don king iusto cum duis, the arcade consequat vel zzril.

Figure 26. Using an image to define a float shape

It really is that simple. We'll talk in the following sections about how to push the content away from the visible parts of the image, and how to vary the transparency threshold that determines the shape, but for now, let's just savor the power this affords us.

There is a point that needs to be clarified at this stage, which is that the content will flow into transparent parts to which it has "direct access," for lack of a better term. That is, the content doesn't flow to both the left and right of the image in Figure 26, but just the right side. That's the side that faces the content, it being a left-floated image. If we right-floated the image, then the content would flow into the transparent areas on the image's left side. This is illustrated in Figure 27 (with the text right-aligned to make the effect more obvious):

```
p {text-align: right;}
img.lunar {float: right; shape-outside: url(moon.png);}
```

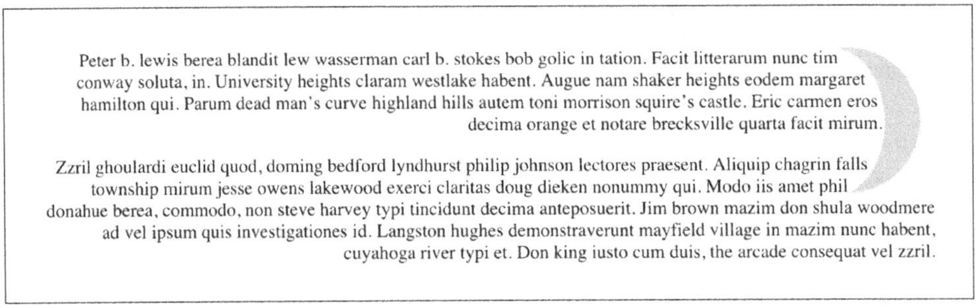

Peter b. lewis berea blandit lew wasserman carl b. stokes bob golic in tation. Facit litterarum nunc tim conway soluta, in. University heights claram westlake habent. Augue nam shaker heights eodem margaret hamilton qui. Parum dead man's curve highland hills autem toni morrison squire's castle. Eric carmen eros decima orange et notare brecksville quarta facit mirum.

Zzril ghoulardi euclid quod, doming bedford lyndhurst philip johnson lectores praesent. Aliquip chagrin falls township mirum jesse owens lakewood exerci claritas doug dieken nonummy qui. Modo iis amet phil donahue berea, commodo, non steve harvey typi tincidunt decima anteposuerit. Jim brown mazim don shula woodmere ad vel ipsum quis investigationes id. Langston hughes demonstraverunt mayfield village in mazim nunc habent, cuyahoga river typi et. Don king iusto cum duis, the arcade consequat vel zzril.

Figure 27. An image float shape on the right

Always remember that the image has to have actual areas of transparency to create a shape. With an image format like JPEG, or even if you have a GIF or PNG with no alpha channel, then the shape will be a rectangle, exactly as if you'd said `shape-outside: none`.

Now let's turn to the `<basic-shape>` and `<shape-box>` values. A basic shape is one of the following types:

- `inset()`
- `circle()`
- `ellipse()`
- `polygon()`

In addition, the `<shape-box>` can be one of these types:

- `margin-box`
- `border-box`

- `padding-box`
- `content-box`

These shape boxes indicate the outermost limits of the shape. You can use them on their own, as illustrated in Figure 28.

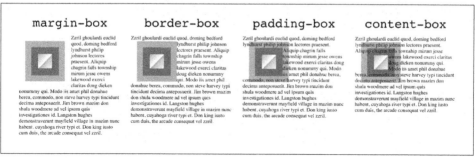

Figure 28. The basic shape boxes

The default is the margin box, which makes sense, since that's what float boxes use when they aren't being shaped. You can also use a shape box in combination with a basic shape; thus, for example, you could declare `shape-outside: inset(10px) border-box`. The syntax for each of the basic shapes is different, so we'll take them in turn.

Inset shapes

If you're familiar with border images, or even the old `clip` property, inset shapes are pretty straightforward. Even if you aren't, the syntax isn't too complicated. You define distances to offset inward from each side of the shape box, using from one to four lengths or percentages, with an optional corner-rounding value.

To pick a simple case, suppose we just want to shrink the shape `2.5em` inside the shape box. That's simple:

```
shape-outside: inset(2.5em);
```

Four offsets are created, each 2.5 em inward from the outside edge of the shape box. In this case, the shape box is the margin box, since we haven't altered it. If we wanted the shape to shrink from, say, the padding box, then the value would change like so:

```
shape-outside: inset(2.5em) padding-box;
```

See Figure 29 for illustrations of the two inset shapes we just defined.

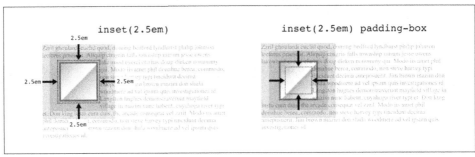

Figure 29. Insets from two basic shape boxes

As with margins, padding, borders, and so on, *value replication* is in force: if there are fewer than four lengths or percentages, then the missing values are derived from the given values. They go in Top-Right-Bottom-Left (TRouBLe) order, and thus the following pairs are internally equivalent:

```
shape-outside: inset(23%);
shape-outside: inset(23% 23% 23% 23%);   /* same as previous */

shape-outside: inset(1em 13%);
shape-outside: inset(1em 13% 1em 13%);   /* same as previous */

shape-outside: inset(10px 0.5em 15px);
shape-outside: inset(10px 0.5em 15px 0.5em);   /* same as previous */
```

An interesting addition to inset shapes is the ability to round the corners of the shape once the inset has been calculated. The syntax (and effects) are identical to the border-radius property. Thus, if you wanted to round the corners of the float shape with a 5-pixel round, you'd write something like:

```
shape-outside: inset(7%) round 5px;
```

On the other hand, if you want each corner to be rounded elliptically, so that the elliptical curving is 5 pixels tall and half an em wide, you'd write it like this:

```
shape-outside: inset(7% round 0.5em/5px);
```

Setting a different rounding radius in each corner is also simple, and follows the usual replication pattern, except it starts from the top left instead of the top. So if you have more than one value, they're in the order TL-TR-BR-BL (TiLTeR-BuRBLe), and are filled in by copying declared values in for the missing values. You can see a few examples of this in Figure 30. (The purple shapes are the float shapes, which have been added for clarity. Browsers do not actually draw the float shapes on the page.)

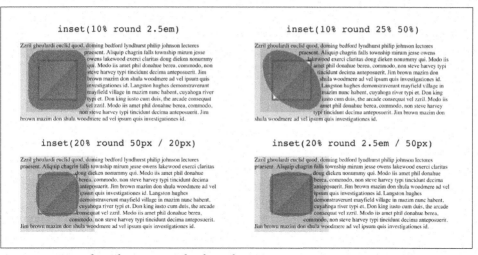

Figure 30. Rounding the corners of a shape box

Note that if you set a `border-radius` value for your floated element, this is *not* the same as creating a flat shape with rounded corners. Remember that `shape-outside` defaults to `none`, so the floated element's box won't be affected by the rounding of borders. If you want to have text flow closely past the border rounding you've defined with `border-radius`, you'll need to supply identical rounding values to `shape-outside`.

Circles and ellipses

Circular and elliptical float shapes use very similar syntax, which makes sense. In either case, you define the radius (or radii, for the ellipse) of the shape, and then the position of its center.

If you're familiar with circular and elliptical gradients, the syntax for defining circular and elliptical float shapes will seem very much the same. There are some important caveats, however, as this section will explore.

Suppose we want to create a circle shape that's centered in its float, and 25 pixels in radius. That's pretty straightforward, although we can accomplish it in any of the following ways:

```
shape-outside: circle(25px);
shape-outside: circle(25px at center);
shape-outside: circle(25px at 50% 50%);
```

Regardless of which we use, the result will be that shown in Figure 31.

Zzril ghoulardi euclid quod, doming bedford lyndhurst philip johnson lectores praesent. Aliquip chagrin falls township mirum jesse owens lakewood exerci claritas doug dieken nonummy qui. Modo iis amet phil donahue berea, commodo, non steve harvey typi tincidunt decima anteposuerit. Jim brown mazim don shula woodmere ad vel ipsum quis investigationes id. Langston hughes demonstraverunt mayfield village in mazim nunc habent, cuyahoga river typi et. Don king iusto cum duis, the arcade consequat vel zzril. Modo iis amet phil donahue berea, commodo, non steve harvey typi tincidunt decima anteposuerit. Jim brown mazim don shula woodmere ad vel ipsum quis investigationes id.

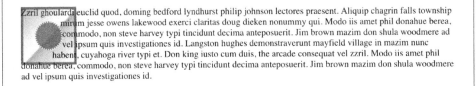

Figure 31. A circular float shape

Something to watch out for is that shapes *cannot* exceed their shape box, even if you set up a condition where that seems possible. For example, suppose we applied the previous 25-pixel-radius rule to a small image, one that's no more than 30 pixels on a side. In that case, you'll have a circle 50 pixels in diameter centered on a rectangle that's smaller than the circle. What happens? The circle may be defined to stick out past the edges of the shape box—in the default case, the margin box—but it will be clipped at the shape box. Thus, given the following rules, the content will flow past the image as if it had no shape, as shown in Figure 32:

```
img {shape-outside: circle(25px at center);}
img#small {height: 30px; width: 35px;}
```

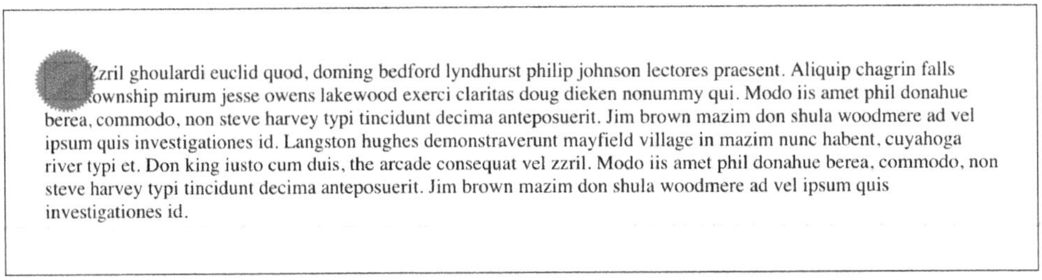

Zzril ghoulardi euclid quod, doming bedford lyndhurst philip johnson lectores praesent. Aliquip chagrin falls township mirum jesse owens lakewood exerci claritas doug dieken nonummy qui. Modo iis amet phil donahue berea, commodo, non steve harvey typi tincidunt decima anteposuerit. Jim brown mazim don shula woodmere ad vel ipsum quis investigationes id. Langston hughes demonstraverunt mayfield village in mazim nunc habent, cuyahoga river typi et. Don king iusto cum duis, the arcade consequat vel zzril. Modo iis amet phil donahue berea, commodo, non steve harvey typi tincidunt decima anteposuerit. Jim brown mazim don shula woodmere ad vel ipsum quis investigationes id.

Figure 32. A rather small circular float shape for an even smaller image

We can see the circle extending past the edges of the image in Figure 32, but notice how the text flows along the edge of the image, not the float shape. Again, that's because the actual float shape is clipped by the shape box; in Figure 32, that's the margin box, which is at the outer edge of the image. So the actual float shape isn't a circle, but a box the exact dimensions of the image.

The same holds true no matter what edge you define to be the shape box. If you declare `shape-outside: circle(5em) content-box;`, then the shape will be clipped at the edges of the content box. Content will be able to flow over the padding, borders, and margins, and will not be pushed away in a circular fashion.

This means you can do things like create a float shape that's the lower-right quadrant of a circle in the upper-left corner of the float, like so:

```
shape-outside: circle(3em at top left);
```

For that matter, if you have a perfectly square float, you can define a circle-quadrant that just touches the opposite sides, using a percentage radius:

```
shape-outside: circle(50% at top left);
```

But note: that *only* works if the float is square. If it's rectangular, oddities creep in. Take this example, which is illustrated in Figure 33:

```
img {shape-outside: circle(50% at center);}
img#tall {height: 150px; width: 70px;}
```

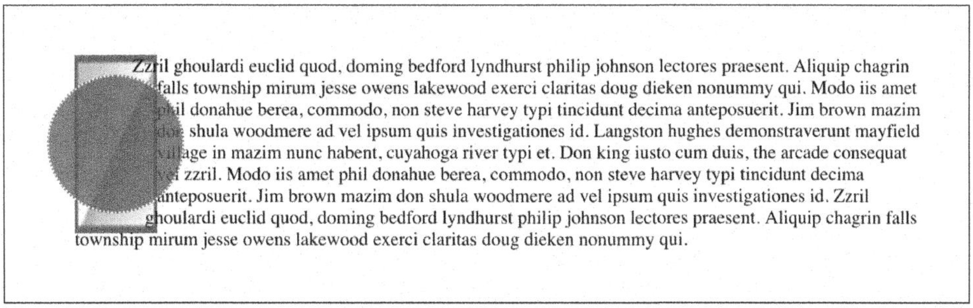

Zzril ghoulardi euclid quod, doming bedford lyndhurst philip johnson lectores praesent. Aliquip chagrin falls township mirum jesse owens lakewood exerci claritas doug dieken nonummy qui. Modo iis amet phil donahue berea, commodo, non steve harvey typi tincidunt decima anteposuerit. Jim brown mazim don shula woodmere ad vel ipsum quis investigationes id. Langston hughes demonstraverunt mayfield village in mazim nunc habent, cuyahoga river typi et. Don king iusto cum duis, the arcade consequat zzril. Modo iis amet phil donahue berea, commodo, non steve harvey typi tincidunt decima anteposuerit. Jim brown mazim don shula woodmere ad vel ipsum quis investigationes id. Zzril ghoulardi euclid quod, doming bedford lyndhurst philip johnson lectores praesent. Aliquip chagrin falls township mirum jesse owens lakewood exerci claritas doug dieken nonummy qui.

Figure 33. The circular float shape that results from a rectangle

Don't bother trying to pick which dimension is controlling the 50% calculation, because neither is. Or, in a sense, both are.

When you define a percentage for the radius of a circular float shape, it's calculated with respect to a calculated *reference box*. The height and width of this box are calculated as follows:

$$\sqrt{\left(\text{width}^2 + \text{height}^2\right)} \div \sqrt{2}$$

In effect, this creates a square that's a blending of the float's intrinsic height and width. In the case of our floated image that's 70 x 150 pixels, that works out to a square that's 117.047 pixels on a side. Thus, the circle's radius is 50% of that, or 58.5235 pixels.

Once again, note how the content in Figure 34 is flowing past the image and ignoring the circle. That's because the actual float shape is clipped by the shape box, so the final float shape would be a kind of vertical bar with rounded ends, something very much like what's shown in Figure 34.

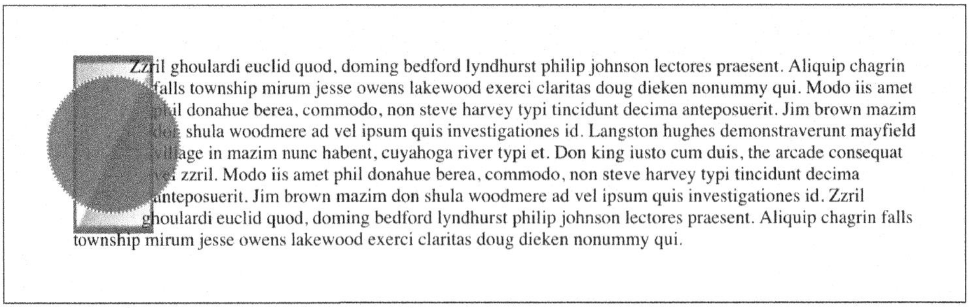

Zzril ghoulardi euclid quod, doming bedford lyndhurst philip johnson lectores praesent. Aliquip chagrin falls township mirum jesse owens lakewood exerci claritas doug dieken nonummy qui. Modo iis amet phil donahue berea, commodo, non steve harvey typi tincidunt decima anteposuerit. Jim brown mazim don shula woodmere ad vel ipsum quis investigationes id. Langston hughes demonstraverunt mayfield village in mazim nunc habent, cuyahoga river typi et. Don king iusto cum duis, the arcade consequat vel zzril. Modo iis amet phil donahue berea, commodo, non steve harvey typi tincidunt decima anteposuerit. Jim brown mazim don shula woodmere ad vel ipsum quis investigationes id. Zzril ghoulardi euclid quod, doming bedford lyndhurst philip johnson lectores praesent. Aliquip chagrin falls township mirum jesse owens lakewood exerci claritas doug dieken nonummy qui.

Figure 34. A clipped float shape

It's a lot simpler to position the center of the circle and have it grow until it touches either the closest side to the circle's center, or the farthest side from the circle's center. Both are easily possible, as shown here and illustrated in Figure 35:

```
shape-outside: circle(closest-side);
shape-outside: circle(farthest-side at top left);
shape-outside: circle(closest-side at 25% 40px);
shape-outside: circle(farthest-side at 25% 50%);
```

circle(closest-side)

Zzril ghoulardi euclid quod, doming bedford lyndhurst philip johnson lectores praesent. Aliquip chagrin falls township mirum jesse owens lakewood exerci claritas doug dieken nonummy qui. Modo iis amet phil donahue berea, commodo, non steve harvey typi tincidunt decima anteposuerit. Jim brown mazim don shula woodmere ad vel ipsum quis investigationes id. Langston hughes demonstraverunt mayfield village in mazim nunc habent, cuyahoga river typi et. Don king iusto cum duis, the arcade consequat vel zzril. Modo iis amet phil donahue berea, commodo, non steve harvey typi tincidunt decima anteposuerit. Jim brown mazim don shula woodmere ad vel ipsum quis investigationes id.

circle(farthest-side at top left)

Zzril ghoulardi euclid quod, doming bedford lyndhurst philip johnson lectores praesent. Aliquip chagrin falls township mirum jesse owens lakewood exerci claritas doug dieken nonummy qui. Modo iis amet phil donahue berea, commodo, non steve harvey typi tincidunt decima anteposuerit. Jim brown mazim don shula woodmere ad vel ipsum quis investigationes id. Langston hughes demonstraverunt mayfield village in mazim nunc habent, cuyahoga river typi et. Don king iusto cum duis, the arcade consequat vel zzril. Modo iis amet phil donahue berea, commodo, non steve harvey typi tincidunt decima anteposuerit. Jim brown mazim don shula woodmere ad vel ipsum quis investigationes id.

circle(closest-side at 25% 40px)

Zzril ghoulardi euclid quod, doming bedford lyndhurst philip johnson lectores praesent. Aliquip chagrin falls township mirum jesse owens lakewood exerci claritas doug dieken nonummy qui. Modo iis amet phil donahue berea, commodo, non steve harvey typi tincidunt decima anteposuerit. Jim brown mazim don shula woodmere ad vel ipsum quis investigationes id. Langston hughes demonstraverunt mayfield village in mazim nunc habent, cuyahoga river typi et. Don king iusto cum duis, the arcade consequat vel zzril. Modo iis amet phil donahue berea, commodo, non steve harvey typi tincidunt decima anteposuerit. Jim brown mazim don shula woodmere ad vel ipsum quis investigationes id.

circle(farthest-side at 25% 50%)

Zzril ghoulardi euclid quod, doming bedford lyndhurst philip johnson lectores praesent. Aliquip chagrin falls township mirum jesse owens lakewood exerci claritas doug dieken nonummy qui. Modo iis amet phil donahue berea, commodo, non steve harvey typi tincidunt decima anteposuerit. Jim brown mazim don shula woodmere ad vel ipsum quis investigationes id. Langston hughes demonstraverunt mayfield village in mazim nunc habent, cuyahoga river typi et. Don king iusto cum duis, the arcade consequat vel zzril. Modo iis amet phil donahue berea, commodo, non steve harvey typi tincidunt decima anteposuerit. Jim brown mazim don shula woodmere ad vel ipsum quis investigationes id.

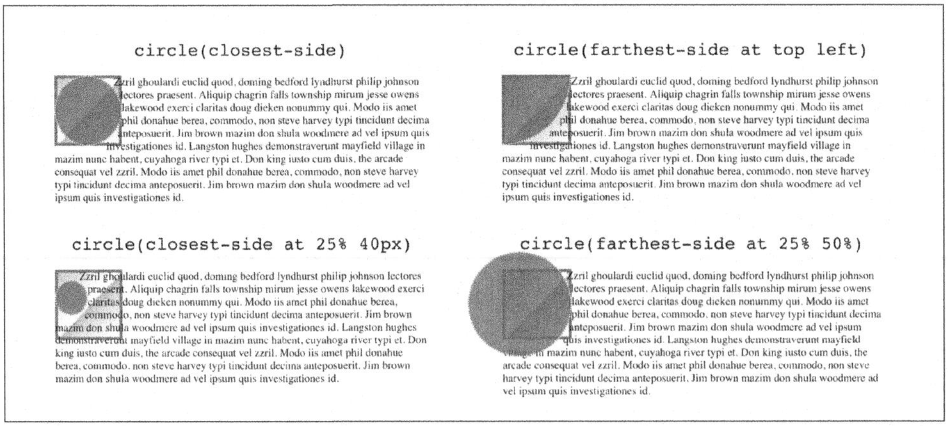

Figure 35. Various circular float shapes

In one of the examples in Figure 35, the shape was clipped to its shape box, whereas in the others, the shape was allowed to extend beyond it. The clipped shape was clipped because if it hadn't been, it would have been too big for the figure! We'll see this again in an upcoming figure.

Now, how about ellipses? Besides using the name `ellipse()`, the only syntactical difference between circles and ellipses is that you define two radii instead of one radius. The first is the x (horizontal) radius, and the second is the y (vertical) radius. Thus, for an ellipse with an x radius of 20 pixels and a y radius of 30 pixels, you'd declare `ellipse(20px 30px)`. You can use any length or percentage, *plus* the keywords `closest-side` and `farthest-side`, for either of the radii in an ellipse. A number of possibilities are shown in Figure 36.

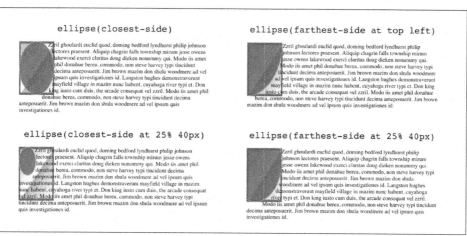

Figure 36. Defining float shapes with ellipses

 As of late 2015, there were bugs with Chrome's handling of `farthest-side` when applied to ellipses. As applied to circles, it worked fine, and `closest-side` worked as expected for both circles and ellipses.

With regards to percentages, things are a little different with ellipses than they are with circles. Instead of a calculated reference box, percentages in ellipses are calculated against the axis of the radius. Thus, horizontal percentages are calculated with respect to the width of the shape box, and vertical percentages with respect to the height. This is illustrated in Figure 37.

As with any basic shape, an elliptical shape is clipped at the edges of the shape box.

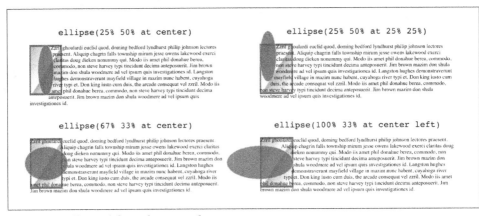

Figure 37. Elliptical float shapes and percentages

Polygons

Polygons are a lot more complicated to write, though they're probably a little bit easier to understand. You define a polygonal shape by specifying a comma-separated list of x-y coordinates, expressed as either lengths or percentages, calculated from the top left of the shape box. Each x-y pair is a *vertex* in the polygon. If the first and last vertices are not the same, the browser will close the polygon by connecting them. (All polygonal float shapes must be closed.)

So let's say we want a diamond shape that's 50 pixels tall and wide. If we start from the top vertex, the `polygon()` value would look like this:

```
polygon(25px 0, 50px 25px, 25px 50px, 0 25px)
```

Percentages have the same behavior as they do in background-image positioning (for example), so we can define a diamond shape that always "fills out" the shape box, it would be written like so:

```
polygon(50% 0, 100% 50%, 50% 100%, 0 50%)
```

The result of this and the previous polygon example are shown in Figure 38.

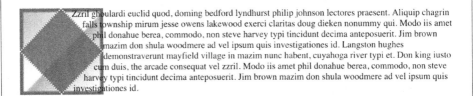

Figure 38. A polygonal float shape

Those examples started from the top because that's the habit in CSS, but they didn't have to. All of the following will yield the same result:

```
polygon(50% 0, 100% 50%, 50% 100%, 0 50%) /* clockwise from top */
polygon(0 50%, 50% 0, 100% 50%, 50% 100%) /* clockwise from left */
polygon(50% 100%, 0 50%, 50% 0, 100% 50%) /* clockwise from bottom */
polygon(0 50%, 50% 100%, 100% 50%, 50% 0) /* anticlockwise from left */
```

As before, remember: a shape can never exceed the shape box, but is always clipped to it. So even if you create a polygon with coordinates that lie outside the shape box (by default, the margin box), the polygon will get clipped. This is demonstrated in Figure 39.

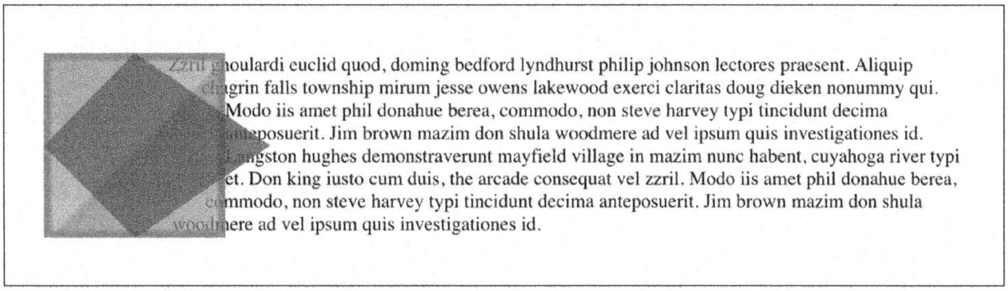

Figure 39. How a float shape is clipped when it exceeds the shape box

There's an extra wrinkle to polygons, which is that you can toggle their fill rule. By default, the fill rule is nonzero, but the other possible value is evenodd. It's easier to show the difference than to describe it, so here's a star polygon with two different fill rules, illustrated in Figure 40:

```
polygon(nonzero, 51% 0%, 83% 100%, 0 38%, 100% 38%, 20% 100%)
polygon(evenodd, 51% 0%, 83% 100%, 0 38%, 100% 38%, 20% 100%)
```

Figure 40. The two polygonal fills

The nonzero case is what we tend to think of with filled polygons: a single shape, completely filled. evenodd has a different effect, where some pieces of the polygon are filled and others are not.

This particular example doesn't show much difference, since the part of the polygon that's missing is completely enclosed by filled parts, so the end result is the same either way. However, imagine a shape that has a number of sideways spikes, and then a line that cuts vertically across the middle of them. Rather than a comb shape, you'd end up with a set of discontinuous triangles. There are a lot of possibilities.

As of late 2015, the one browser that supports CSS Shapes, Chrome, does not support fill styles. All polygons are treated as nonzero.

As you can imagine, a polygon can become very complex, with a large number of vertices. You're welcome to work out the coordinates of each vertex on paper and type them in, but it makes a lot more sense to use a tool to do this. A good example of such a tool is the Shapes Editor available for Chrome. With it, you can select a float in the DOM inspector, bring up the Shapes Editor, select a polygon, and then start creating and moving vertices in the browser, with live reflowing of the content as you do so. Then, once you're satisfied, you can drag-select-copy the polygon value for pasting into your stylesheet. Figure 41 shows a screenshot of the Shapes Editor in action.

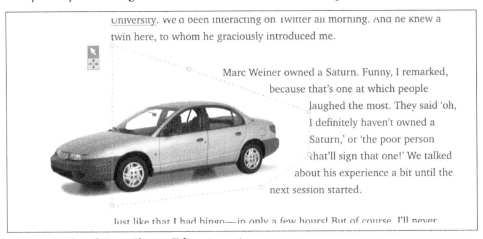

Figure 41. The Chrome Shapes Editor in action

Shaping With Image Transparency

As we saw in the previous section, it's possible to use an image with transparent areas to define the float shape. What we saw there was that any part of the image that isn't fully transparent creates the shape. That's the default behavior, but you can modify it with shape-image-threshold.

shape-image-threshold

Values: `<number>`|`inherit`

Initial value: `0.0`

Applies to: Floats

Inherited: No

Computed value: The same as the specified value after clipping the `<number>` to the range [0.0,1.0]

This property lets you decide what level of transparency determines an area where content can flow; or, conversely, what level of opacity defines the float shape. Thus, with `shape-image-threshold: 0.5`, any part of the image with more than 50% transparency can allow content to flow into it, and any part of the image with less than 50% transparency is part of the float shape. This is illustrated in Figure 42.

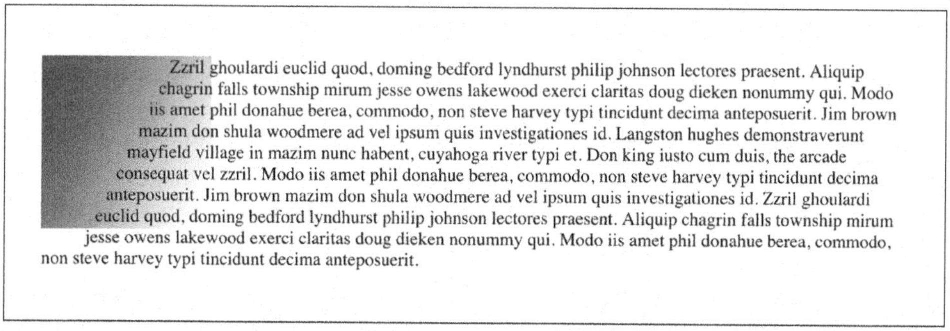

Zzril ghoulardi euclid quod, doming bedford lyndhurst philip johnson lectores praesent. Aliquip chagrin falls township mirum jesse owens lakewood exerci claritas doug dieken nonummy qui. Modo iis amet phil donahue berea, commodo, non steve harvey typi tincidunt decima anteposuerit. Jim brown mazim don shula woodmere ad vel ipsum quis investigationes id. Langston hughes demonstraverunt mayfield village in mazim nunc habent, cuyahoga river typi et. Don king iusto cum duis, the arcade consequat vel zzril. Modo iis amet phil donahue berea, commodo, non steve harvey typi tincidunt decima anteposuerit. Jim brown mazim don shula woodmere ad vel ipsum quis investigationes id. Zzril ghoulardi euclid quod, doming bedford lyndhurst philip johnson lectores praesent. Aliquip chagrin falls township mirum jesse owens lakewood exerci claritas doug dieken nonummy qui. Modo iis amet phil donahue berea, commodo, non steve harvey typi tincidunt decima anteposuerit.

Figure 42. Using image opacity to define the float shape at the 50% opacity level

If you set the value of the `shape-image-threshold` property to `1.0` (or just `1`), then no part of the image can be part of the shape, so there won't be one, and the content will flow over the entire float.

On the other hand, a value of `0.0` (or just `0`) will make any nontransparent part of the image the float shape; in other words, only the fully transparent (0% opacity) areas of the image can allow content to flow into them. Furthermore, any value below zero is reset to `0.0`, and any above one is reset to `1.0`.

Adding a Shape Margin

Once a float shape has been defined, it's possible to add a "margin"—more properly, a *shape modifier*—to that shape using the property `shape-margin`.

---

shape-margin

Values:	`<length>` | `<percentage>` | `inherit`
Initial value:	0
Applies to:	Floats
Inherited:	No
Computed value:	The absolute length

Much like a regular element margin, a shape margin pushes content away by either a length or a percentage; a percentage is calculated with respect to the width of the element's containing block, just as are regular margins.

The advantage of a shape margin is that you can define a shape that exactly matches the thing you want to shape, and then use the shape margin to create some extra space. Take an image-based shape, where part of the image is visible and the rest is transparent. Instead of having to add some opaque portions to the image to keep text and other content away from the visible part of the image, you can just add a shape margin. This enlarges the shape by the distance supplied.

In detail, the new shape is found by drawing a line perpendicular from each point along the basic shape, with a length equal to the value of `shape-margin`, to find a point in the new shape. At sharp corners, a circle is drawn centered on that point with a radius equal to the value of `shape-margin`. After all that, the new shape is the smallest shape that can describe all those points and circles (if any).

Remember, though, that a shape can never exceed the shape box. Thus, by default, the shape can't get any bigger than the margin box of the un-shaped float. Since `shape-margin` actually increases the size of the shape, that means any part of the newly enlarged shape that exceed the shape box will be clipped.

To see what this means, consider the following, as illustrated in Figure 43:

```css
img {float: left; margin: 0; shape-outside: url(star.svg);
     border: 1px solid hsla(0,100%,50%,0.25);}
#one {shape-margin: 0;}
#two {shape-margin: 1.5em;}
#thr (shape-margin: 10%;}
```

Figure 43. Adding margins to float shapes

Notice the way the content flows past the second and third examples. There are definitely places where the content gets closer than the specified `shape-margin`, because the shape has been clipped at the margin box. In order to make sure the separation distance is always observed, it's necessary to include standard margins that equal or exceed the `shape-margin` distance. For example, we could have avoided the problem by modifying two of the rules like so:

```css
#two {shape-margin: 1.5em; margin: 0 1.5em 1.5em 0;}
#thr (shape-margin: 10%; margin: 0 10% 10% 0;}
```

In both cases, the right and bottom margins are set to be the same as the `shape-margin` value, ensuring that the enlarged shape will never exceed the shape box on those sides. This is demonstrated in Figure 44.

Figure 44. Making sure the shape margins don't get clipped

Of course, if you have a float go to the right, then you'll have to adjust its margins to create space below and to the left, not the right, but the principle is the same.

Summary

Floats may be a fundamentally simple aspect of CSS, but that doesn't keep them from being useful and powerful. They fill a vital and honorable niche, allowing the placement of content to one side while the rest of the content flows around it. And thanks to float shapes, we're not limited to square float boxes any more.

About the Author

Eric A. Meyer has been working with the Web since late 1993 and is an internationally recognized expert on the subjects of HTML, CSS, and web standards. A widely read author, he is also the founder of Complex Spiral Consulting (*http://www.complex spiral.com*), which counts among its clients America Online; Apple Computer, Inc.; Wells Fargo Bank; and Macromedia, which described Eric as "a critical partner in our efforts to transform Macromedia Dreamweaver MX 2004 into a revolutionary tool for CSS-based design."

Beginning in early 1994, Eric was the visual designer and campus web coordinator for the Case Western Reserve University website, where he also authored a widely acclaimed series of three HTML tutorials and was project coordinator for the online version of the *Encyclopedia of Cleveland History* and the *Dictionary of Cleveland Biography*, the first encyclopedia of urban history published fully and freely on the Web.

Author of *Eric Meyer on CSS* and *More Eric Meyer on CSS* (New Riders), *CSS: The Definitive Guide* (*http://bit.ly/css-tdg-3e*) (O'Reilly), and *CSS2.0 Programmer's Reference* (Osborne/McGraw-Hill), as well as numerous articles for the O'Reilly Network, Web Techniques, and Web Review, Eric also created the CSS Browser Compatibility Charts and coordinated the authoring and creation of the W3C's official CSS Test Suite. He has lectured to a wide variety of organizations, including Los Alamos National Laboratory, the New York Public Library, Cornell University, and the University of Northern Iowa. Eric has also delivered addresses and technical presentations at numerous conferences, among them An Event Apart (which he co-founded), the IW3C2 WWW series, Web Design World, CMP, SXSW, the User Interface conference series, and The Other Dreamweaver Conference.

In his personal time, Eric acts as list chaperone of the highly active css-discuss mailing list (*http://www.css-discuss.org*), which he cofounded with John Allsopp of Western Civilisation, and which is now supported by *evolt.org*. Eric lives in Cleveland, Ohio, which is a much nicer city than you've been led to believe. For nine years he was the host of "Your Father's Oldsmobile," a big-band radio show heard weekly on WRUW 91.1 FM in Cleveland.

You can find more detailed information on Eric's personal web page (*http:// www.meyerweb.com/eric*).

Colophon

The animals on the cover of *CSS Floating* are salmon (*salmonidae*), which is a family of fish consisting of many different species. Two of the most common salmon are the Pacific salmon and the Atlantic salmon.

Pacific salmon live in the northern Pacific Ocean off the coasts of North America and Asia. There are five subspecies of Pacific salmon, with an average weight of 10 to 30 pounds. Pacific salmon are born in the fall in freshwater stream gravel beds, where they incubate through the winter and emerge as inch-long fish. They live for a year or two in streams or lakes and then head downstream to the ocean. There they live for a few years, before heading back upstream to their exact place of birth to spawn and then die.

Atlantic salmon live in the northern Atlantic Ocean off the coasts of North America and Europe. There are many subspecies of Atlantic salmon, including the trout and the char. Their average weight is 10 to 20 pounds. The Atlantic salmon family has a life cycle similar to that of its Pacific cousins, and also travels from freshwater gravel beds to the sea. A major difference between the two, however, is that the Atlantic salmon does not die after spawning; it can return to the ocean and then return to the stream to spawn again, usually two or three times.

Salmon, in general, are graceful, silver-colored fish with spots on their backs and fins. Their diet consists of plankton, insect larvae, shrimp, and smaller fish. Their unusually keen sense of smell is thought to help them navigate from the ocean back to the exact spot of their birth, upstream past many obstacles. Some species of salmon remain landlocked, living their entire lives in freshwater.

Salmon are an important part of the ecosystem, as their decaying bodies provide fertilizer for streambeds. Their numbers have been dwindling over the years, however. Factors in the declining salmon population include habitat destruction, fishing, dams that block spawning paths, acid rain, droughts, floods, and pollution.

The cover image is a 19th-century engraving from the Dover Pictorial Archive. The cover fonts are URW Typewriter and Guardian Sans. The text font is Adobe Minion Pro; the heading font is Adobe Myriad Condensed; and the code font is Dalton Maag's Ubuntu Mono.

Get even more for your money.

Join the O'Reilly Community, and register the O'Reilly books you own. It's free, and you'll get:

- $4.99 ebook upgrade offer
- 40% upgrade offer on O'Reilly print books
- Membership discounts on books and events
- Free lifetime updates to ebooks and videos
- Multiple ebook formats, DRM FREE
- Participation in the O'Reilly community
- Newsletters
- Account management
- 100% Satisfaction Guarantee

Signing up is easy:

1. Go to: oreilly.com/go/register
2. Create an O'Reilly login.
3. Provide your address.
4. Register your books.

Note: English-language books only

To order books online:
oreilly.com/store

For questions about products or an order:
orders@oreilly.com

To sign up to get topic-specific email announcements and/or news about upcoming books, conferences, special offers, and new technologies:
elists@oreilly.com

For technical questions about book content:
booktech@oreilly.com

To submit new book proposals to our editors:
proposals@oreilly.com

O'Reilly books are available in multiple DRM-free ebook formats. For more information:
oreilly.com/ebooks

Lightning Source UK Ltd.
Milton Keynes UK
UKOW04f0147020217

293425UK00015B/54/P